The Beginner SEO Guide for Small Local Business Owners

Roggie Clark

Master SEO With This One Book

https://www.amazon.com/ABCs-Search-Engine-Optimization-Page-ebook

Checkout These Books to Learn More SEO From Me

Creating An SEO Strategy 101: Learn How to Create An Effective SEO Content, Website and Link-Building Strategy From Scratch

https://www.amazon.com/Creating-SEO-Strategy-101-Link-Building-ebook

Technical SEO Handbook: Learn How to Audit and Fix Advanced Technical SEO Issues

https://www.amazon.com/Technical-SEO-Handbook-Learn-Issues-ebook

Copyright

Title: The Beginner SEO Guide for Small Local Business Owners
Author: Roggie Clark

Published by Kindle Direct Publishing
410 Terry Ave N
Seattle, Washington, 98109
United States
https://kdp.amazon.com/en_US

Cover Design: Roggie Clark

Editing: Renee' Clark

ISBN: 979-8-218-19232-7

Printed in the United States of America

Disclaimer

The views and opinions expressed in this book are those of the author and do not necessarily reflect the official policy or position of any individual, company, or organization cited or referenced in the text. The author is not affiliated with any of the individuals, companies, or organizations mentioned in the text, nor does the author receive any form of compensation for citing or referencing them. Some sample scenarios in this text are fictitious. Any similarity to actual persons, living or dead, is coincidental.

The professional information (strategies, tips, and concepts) in this text is distributed on an "as is" basis, without warranty. While every precaution has been taken in the preparation of the text to ensure all information is accurate, neither the author nor the publisher shall have any liability to any person or entity with respect to any loss or damage caused or alleged to be caused directly or indirectly by the instructions contained in this text or by the computer software and hardware products described in it.

The author nor the publisher guarantees any specific results or outcomes, and the information provided in this text should not be construed as professional advice. Readers should always consult with a qualified professional before making any significant changes to their website or business.

By reading this text, you agree that the author nor the publisher is responsible for any direct, indirect, incidental, or consequential damages that may arise from the use of the information provided. You assume full responsibility for any actions taken based on the information presented in this text.

Table of Contents

Introduction

First and foremost, thank you for choosing this book.

I do not take it lightly that you decided to invest your time into learning SEO for your small local business. There are countless marketing books, courses, videos, and "gurus" promising fast rankings and instant results. I am fully aware of that.

But here is the reality.

If you are a small local business owner, you do not need complicated strategies. You do not need a 200 page technical manual. And you certainly do not need someone promising you guaranteed page one rankings.

What you need is clarity.

You need to understand how local search works, why some businesses consistently show up in your city while others remain invisible, and what practical steps you can take to improve your visibility without turning yourself into a full time marketer.

That is what this book is about.

How This Book Is Different

Most SEO books are written for agencies, bloggers, or digital marketers. They often assume you already understand technical terminology. They may dive into complex coding topics, algorithm updates, or advanced link acquisition strategies.

This book does not do that.

The Beginner SEO Guide for Small Local Business Owners was written specifically for business owners who:

- Run a brick and mortar location
- Offer services in a defined geographic area
- Depend on nearby customers
- Do not have a full time marketing team

You will not find "secret hacks" in these pages.

You will find structure.

You will find principles.

You will find practical steps that are realistic for a busy business owner who is already juggling operations, customer service, payroll, and everything else that comes with running a company.

Local SEO Is Not Optional Anymore

There was a time when word of mouth and physical signage were enough.

That time is gone.

Today, when someone needs a plumber, dentist, landscaper, restaurant, or auto repair shop, they do not flip through a phone book. They open their phone and type:

"plumber near me"

"best dentist in my city"

"pizza open now"

If your business does not appear in those results, you are invisible in that moment.

And those moments are high intent moments.

These are not casual browsers scrolling social media for entertainment. These are people actively searching for a solution. They have a problem. They want it solved. And they are ready to take action.

Understanding how to position your business in those moments can dramatically impact your revenue.

How Local SEO Is Different From Traditional SEO

Before we go further, it is important to clarify something.

Local SEO is not the same as general SEO.

Traditional SEO often focuses on ranking nationally or globally. Local SEO focuses on geographic relevance.

When someone searches for "dentist," Google does not show dentists across the country. It shows dentists near the searcher.

This means proximity, relevance, and trust signals play a major role.

As you read this book, you will begin to see how location, reviews, website structure, and consistency across directories all work together to influence local rankings.

How To Use This Book

I recommend that you read this book from beginning to end before trying to implement everything at once.

SEO, even local SEO, is like a system. If you attempt to change everything simultaneously without understanding how the pieces connect, you may create confusion or inconsistencies.

Take your time.

As you read:

- Highlight sections that apply directly to your business
- Write down questions
- Make notes about improvements you already know you need
- Resist the urge to rush

Local SEO is not about speed. It is about structure and consistency.

You may also find it helpful to treat this book as a working manual. When you reach the action plan chapter, you can revisit earlier chapters and apply them step by step.

The Long Term Mindset

One final thing before we begin.

SEO is not advertising.

Advertising stops when you stop paying.

SEO builds an asset.

When done properly, local SEO strengthens your visibility month after month. Reviews accumulate. Content builds authority. Your business profile becomes more complete. Your website becomes clearer and more relevant.

The goal is not a quick spike.

The goal is stable visibility.

Last Thoughts

My intention with this book is not to overwhelm you. It is to simplify a subject that has become unnecessarily complicated.

Local SEO is not magic. It is not manipulation. And it is not about tricking search engines.

It is about making your business easier to find, easier to understand, and easier to trust.

If you are willing to approach it with patience and structure, the results can compound over time.

Let's move into Chapter 1, where we will break down how local search actually works and why some businesses consistently appear at the top of the results in your city.

Chapter 1: How Local Search Actually Works

Before you can improve your rankings, you need to understand what is actually happening behind the scenes.

Most business owners think search results are random. They assume Google simply "chooses" businesses at the top. That is not how it works.

Local search operates on a structured system. When someone types in a query, there is a process taking place in fractions of a second. That process determines which businesses appear, in what order, and in which format.

If you understand that system, you stop guessing.
You start positioning.

Let's break it down.

What Happens When Someone Searches for a Local Service

Imagine someone types:

"plumber near me"

Here is what happens instantly:

1. Google detects the user's location.

2. Google analyzes the intent of the query.

3. Google scans its index for businesses relevant to that service in that geographic area.

4. Google ranks those businesses based on multiple local ranking factors.

This is not the same as a national search.

If someone searches for “how to fix a leaking pipe,” Google may show blog articles or instructional videos. But when someone searches “plumber near me,” Google understands that the intent is transactional. The user wants to hire someone.

That difference matters.

Local search is heavily driven by intent and proximity.

If you internalize this process, you begin to see why certain optimizations matter.

Understanding the Local Map Pack

When you search for a service, you have likely noticed a box at the top of the results showing three businesses with a map.

This is called the Local Map Pack.

It is prime digital real estate.

The Map Pack typically includes:

- Business name
- Star rating
- Number of reviews
- Address
- Phone number
- Hours
- Website link
- Directions

For local businesses, appearing in the Map Pack can generate:

- Phone calls
- Direction requests
- Website visits

- Immediate customer inquiries

In many industries, the Map Pack receives more clicks than traditional organic listings.

Understanding how to influence Map Pack visibility is one of the core objectives of local SEO.

Organic Results vs Map Listings

Below the Map Pack, you will usually see traditional organic results.

These are website pages ranked through broader SEO signals such as:

- Website content
- Backlinks
- Technical structure
- On page optimization

The Map Pack is influenced more heavily by:

- Google Business Profile optimization

- Reviews
- Proximity
- Citation consistency
- Local relevance

This means you are effectively optimizing for two systems:

1. The Local Map algorithm
2. The Organic search algorithm

They overlap, but they are not identical.

Some businesses rank in the Map Pack but not organically.
Some rank organically but not in the Map Pack.
The strongest businesses tend to appear in both.

That is the goal.

Proximity, Relevance, and Authority Explained

Google has publicly stated that local rankings are primarily influenced by three pillars:

- Proximity

- Relevance
- Prominence

Let's simplify them.

Proximity refers to how close your business is to the searcher.
You cannot control where the searcher is located. But you can make sure Google clearly understands where you are located.

Relevance refers to how well your business matches the query.

If someone searches "emergency plumber," and your profile clearly indicates emergency plumbing services, you are more relevant.

Prominence refers to how well known and trusted your business appears online.
This includes:

- Reviews
- Mentions across the web
- Backlinks

- Brand recognition

If one pillar is weak, rankings suffer.

Local SEO is about strengthening all three.

Why Some Small Businesses Rank and Others Do Not

This is where many business owners become frustrated.

They assume ranking is about luck.

It is not.

Businesses that rank consistently tend to:

- Have fully optimized Google Business Profiles
- Maintain accurate and consistent contact information
- Collect steady reviews
- Have structured service pages on their websites
- Display clear location signals
- Earn local mentions and backlinks

Businesses that struggle often:

- Leave profiles incomplete
- Have inconsistent addresses across directories
- Ignore reviews
- Have thin website content
- Lack clear service descriptions

Local search is not random.

It rewards clarity and consistency.

The good news is this:

You do not need to outspend competitors.
You need to out organize them.

Last Thoughts on How Local Search Works

Local search is structured, intent driven, and location sensitive.

It is not about gaming the system. It is about aligning your business with how the system works.

When someone searches for a service in your area, Google is trying to answer one question:

"Which business is most likely to solve this person's problem right now?"

If your business sends clear signals that you are relevant, trustworthy, and located nearby, you increase your chances of being selected.

Now that you understand how local search works, we can move into the next critical step:

Setting up and optimizing your Google Business Profile properly, which is the foundation of strong local visibility.

Chapter 2: Setting Up and Optimizing Your Google Business Profile

If local SEO were a house, your Google Business Profile would be the foundation.

You can have a beautiful website.
You can have strong content.
You can even have backlinks.

But if your Google Business Profile is incomplete, inconsistent, or poorly optimized, you are weakening your local visibility before you even begin.

For small local business owners, this is the single most important asset in local search.

Let's break it down properly.

Claiming and Verifying Your Business

Before you optimize anything, you need ownership.

If you have not claimed your Google Business Profile, you do not control your digital storefront.

To get started:

1. Search your business name on Google.
2. If a profile appears, look for the "Own this business?" link.

3. Follow the verification steps provided by Google.

Verification usually happens through:

- Postcard mailed to your business address
- Phone verification
- Email verification
- Video verification

Without verification, you cannot fully edit or optimize your listing.

This step is non negotiable.

If you skip this step, everything else in this chapter becomes irrelevant.

Once verified, you are officially in control.

Choosing the Right Primary and Secondary Categories

This is one of the most misunderstood parts of local SEO.

Your primary category tells Google what your business is.

Not what you "kind of do."
Not what you "also offer."
What you are.

If you are a plumbing company, your primary category should likely be “Plumber.” Not “Home Services.” Not “Contractor.”

The primary category carries significant ranking weight.

Then you can add secondary categories to support additional services.

For example, a plumbing business might add:

- Drain cleaning service
- Water heater installation service
- Emergency plumbing service

Be precise.

Choosing the wrong primary category can dramatically reduce your visibility for high intent searches.

When in doubt, search your top keyword and look at the categories used by businesses already ranking in the Map Pack.

Patterns usually reveal themselves quickly.

Writing a Clear and Keyword Focused Business Description

Your business description is not a place for fluff.

It is not a place for generic marketing language like:

"We are committed to excellence and customer satisfaction."

That tells Google nothing.

Your description should clearly state:

- What you do
- Who you serve
- Where you serve

For example:

"We provide residential and commercial plumbing services in Dallas, Texas, including emergency plumbing repairs, drain cleaning, and water heater installation."

That is clear.
That is location specific.
That aligns with search intent.

Avoid keyword stuffing. Write naturally. But be intentional.

You are helping both users and search engines understand your business.

Uploading Photos That Improve Engagement

Most business owners underestimate the power of images.

Photos influence:

- Click through rate
- Customer trust
- Engagement signals
- Perceived legitimacy

Upload:

- Exterior photos
- Interior photos
- Team photos
- Service photos
- Before and after examples
- Branded vehicles

Google wants active businesses.

Profiles with consistent updates and fresh images often perform better than stagnant listings.

Your profile should not look abandoned.

Business Hours, Services, and Attributes

Incomplete profiles lose trust.

Make sure your hours are accurate. Especially holiday hours.

Add detailed service descriptions inside the Services section.

Use attributes where applicable:

- Women owned
- Veteran owned
- Wheelchair accessible
- Online appointments available

These details help Google match your business to specific search queries.

Clarity increases relevance.

Avoiding Common Profile Mistakes

Many businesses unknowingly damage their own rankings.

Here are common errors to avoid:

- Inconsistent business name formatting
- Adding keywords to your business name that are not part of your legal name
- Using a virtual office address
- Selecting too many irrelevant categories
- Ignoring reviews
- Letting incorrect information remain live

Google's local algorithm rewards consistency and accuracy.

Trying to "game" the system often backfires.

If you would not put it on your storefront sign, do not put it in your business name field.

Why Your Google Business Profile Impacts Rankings So Heavily

Your Google Business Profile directly influences:

- Map Pack visibility
- Branded searches
- Direction requests
- Phone calls
- Review generation
- Local authority

It is not optional.

It is not secondary.

For many local businesses, it drives more leads than their actual website.

If you optimize nothing else in this book but this chapter, you will already be ahead of many competitors.

Last Thoughts on Google Business Profile Optimization

Your Google Business Profile is your digital storefront.

If someone searches for your service in your city, this is often the first impression they see.

An incomplete profile signals inattention.

A fully optimized profile signals professionalism.

Remember this:

Local SEO is not about tricks.
It is about clarity.

When your profile clearly communicates who you are, what you do, and where you operate, you make it easier for Google to confidently recommend you.

Now that your foundation is set, let's move into the next layer:

Building a website that supports and strengthens your local rankings.

Let's move into Chapter 3.

Chapter 3: Building a Website That Supports Local Rankings

There is a growing myth that local businesses no longer need websites.

Some believe that a Google Business Profile alone is enough.

That is not entirely true.

While your Google Business Profile is powerful, your website is what reinforces authority, relevance, and credibility. It is the asset you control. It is the platform where you can fully explain your services, structure your content properly, and build long term search equity.

Think of it this way:

Your Google Business Profile attracts attention.
Your website builds confidence.

Let's break down how to build one that supports your local rankings.

Why Every Local Business Still Needs a Website

Even if customers find you through the Map Pack, many will click your website before calling.

They are looking for:

- Service details
- Pricing information
- Proof of expertise
- Photos of your work
- Testimonials
- Signs of legitimacy

A weak or outdated website can reduce conversions, even if your rankings are strong.

From an SEO perspective, your website helps:

- Strengthen geographic signals
- Reinforce service relevance
- Earn backlinks
- Provide structured content for search engines

Without a strong website, you are limiting your long term growth.

Your website is your digital headquarters.

Structuring Your Homepage for Local Relevance

Your homepage should immediately answer three questions:

1. What do you do?
2. Where do you do it?
3. Why should someone choose you?

Too many local websites make visitors guess.

Your homepage should clearly state your primary service and location near the top of the page.

For example:

"Residential and Commercial Plumbing Services in Phoenix, Arizona"

That is clear.
That is location specific.
That aligns with search intent.

Your homepage should also include:

- A brief overview of core services
- A clear call to action
- Trust indicators such as reviews or certifications
- Consistent Name, Address, and Phone Number

Clarity reduces friction. Friction reduces conversions.

Creating Service Pages That Target Specific Locations

This is where many local businesses fall short.

Instead of listing all services on one page, you should create separate service pages.

For example, a plumbing company should not just have one generic "Services" page. It should have:

- Water Heater Installation
- Drain Cleaning
- Emergency Plumbing
- Leak Detection

Each service page should:

- Clearly describe the service
- Mention the city or service area naturally
- Include FAQs related to that service
- Include strong calls to action

If you serve multiple cities, you may also consider creating location specific pages, but only if you can make them unique and valuable.

Thin, duplicated location pages often do more harm than good.

Quality always beats quantity.

On Page SEO Basics for Beginners

On page SEO simply means optimizing the elements on your website pages to help search engines understand them better.

Here are foundational elements you should focus on:

- Title tags that include your service and location
- Meta descriptions that encourage clicks
- Clear H1 and H2 headings

- Descriptive URLs
- Internal links between related pages

For example, a service page title tag might look like:

“Emergency Plumber in Tampa, Florida | 24 Hour Plumbing Services”

That tells both users and search engines exactly what the page is about.

You do not need to overcomplicate this.

Be clear.
Be specific.
Be consistent.

Mobile Friendliness and Page Speed

Most local searches happen on mobile devices.

If your website loads slowly or is difficult to navigate on a phone, you are losing potential customers.

Google also uses mobile first indexing, meaning it evaluates your mobile experience first.

Make sure:

- Text is readable without zooming
- Buttons are easy to click
- Pages load quickly

- Contact information is clickable

A fast, mobile friendly website improves both rankings and conversions.

User experience is no longer optional.

Clear Calls to Action That Convert Visitors

SEO gets people to your website.

Conversion turns visitors into customers.

Every important page should clearly tell visitors what to do next:

- Call now
- Request a quote
- Schedule an appointment
- Book online

Your phone number should be visible.

Your contact form should be simple.

Your messaging should be direct.

Do not make people search for how to contact you.

When someone searches for a local service, they are often ready to act.

Your website should make that easy.

Last Thoughts on Building a Website for Local SEO

Your website is not just a brochure.

It is a signal.

It signals relevance.
It signals professionalism.
It signals authority.

A well structured website strengthens your Google Business Profile. It reinforces your local presence. It increases trust.

You do not need a flashy design.

You need clarity, structure, and consistency.

Now that your website foundation is in place, the next step is understanding how to choose the right keywords for your local market.

Let's move into Chapter 4.

Chapter 4: Local Keyword Research Made Simple

If your Google Business Profile is the foundation, and your website is the structure, then keywords are the blueprint.

Without the right keywords, everything else becomes guesswork.

Many small business owners make one critical mistake: they assume they know what their customers are searching for.

Assumptions are dangerous in SEO.

Keyword research removes assumptions and replaces them with clarity.

Let's simplify this process.

How to Think Like Your Customer

Before you touch any tools, you need to shift your mindset.

Stop thinking like a business owner.
Start thinking like a customer.

A business owner might say:
"We specialize in hydro jetting services."

A customer might search:
"clogged drain repair near me"

Those are not the same thing.

Customers search using problems, not technical terminology.

Ask yourself:

- What problem is my customer trying to solve?
- What words would they use?
- Would they search broadly or specifically?

When in doubt, keep it simple.

If you are a dentist, your customers are not searching "oral hygiene optimization provider." They are searching "dentist near me" or "teeth cleaning appointment."

SEO rewards clarity.

Finding Service Plus Location Keywords

Local SEO revolves around combining your service with your location.

This is often called a "service + location" keyword structure.

Examples include:

- Plumber in Austin
- Roofing contractor in Denver
- Personal injury lawyer in Atlanta
- Hair salon in Miami

This structure tells Google two things clearly:

1. What you do
2. Where you do it

Start by listing your core services.

Then combine each service with:

- Your city
- Your surrounding cities
- Your neighborhood
- "Near me" variations

For example:

- Emergency plumber Dallas
- Drain cleaning Dallas
- 24 hour plumber near me
- Plumbing repair in Plano

These are high intent searches.

This is the backbone of local keyword research.

Long Tail Keywords for Small Markets

Many small businesses try to rank for broad keywords only.

For example:
"plumber"

That is highly competitive.

Instead, focus on long tail keywords.

Long tail keywords are more specific phrases that often indicate higher intent.

Examples:

- 24 hour emergency plumber in Dallas
- Water heater replacement cost in Tampa
- Affordable drain cleaning in Phoenix

These keywords may have lower search volume individually, but they are:

- Easier to rank for
- More targeted
- Often closer to conversion

Small markets benefit greatly from long tail strategies.

You do not need thousands of searches.
You need the right searches.

Using Free Tools to Discover Search Terms

You do not need expensive software to begin.

Start with:

Google Autocomplete
Google's "People also ask" section
Related searches at the bottom of Google
Google Trends

Simply begin typing your service into Google and observe what appears.

For example, type:

"roof repair…"

You may see suggestions like:

- Roof repair near me
- Roof repair cost
- Roof repair after storm
- Roof repair estimate

These suggestions exist because people are searching them.

Pay attention to patterns.

If multiple suggestions include "cost," that indicates price transparency matters to customers.

If multiple suggestions include "near me," proximity is dominant.

Let Google's own interface guide you.

Matching Search Intent With the Right Page

One of the biggest mistakes small businesses make is creating one generic page and expecting it to rank for everything.

Search intent matters.

If someone searches:

"emergency plumber near me"

They expect:

- Immediate service
- Fast response
- Clear phone number

If someone searches:

"how much does drain cleaning cost"

They expect:

- Informational content
- Pricing guidance
- Transparent explanation

Those are different intents.

Different intents require different pages.

A strong local SEO strategy matches:

- Service pages with transactional keywords
- Blog or FAQ pages with informational keywords

Google rewards relevance.

If your page clearly satisfies the searcher's intent, your chances of ranking improve significantly.

Avoiding Common Keyword Mistakes

Let's simplify what not to do:

- Do not stuff keywords unnaturally into content
- Do not target cities you do not serve
- Do not create duplicate location pages with identical content
- Do not chase high volume keywords that are unrealistic

Keyword research is not about ego.

It is about alignment.

Choose keywords that are:

- Relevant to your services
- Realistic for your market
- Closely aligned with user intent

That is how small businesses compete effectively.

Last Thoughts on Local Keyword Research

Keywords are not about tricking search engines.

They are about understanding how your customers search.

When you align your content with real search behavior, you reduce friction.

- You become easier to find.
- You become easier to understand.
- You become easier to choose.

Now that you understand how to identify the right keywords, we move into something that directly impacts both rankings and trust:

Reviews, reputation, and authority.

Let's move into Chapter 5.

Chapter 5: Reviews, Reputation, and Trust Signals

If keywords drive visibility, reviews drive decisions.

You can rank at the top of the Map Pack.
You can appear on page one organically.
But if your reviews are weak, outdated, or nonexistent, conversions suffer.

Local SEO is not just about ranking.

It is about trust.

When customers search for a local service, they are not only asking, “Who is nearby?” They are asking, “Who can I trust?”

Reviews answer that question instantly.

Why Reviews Impact Rankings and Conversions

Reviews influence two major things:

- Visibility
- Consumer behavior

From a ranking perspective, reviews signal activity and credibility. Businesses with steady review growth often perform better than stagnant listings.

From a conversion perspective, reviews are social proof.

When someone sees:

4.8 stars with 187 reviews

That communicates stability and reliability.

When someone sees:

3 reviews from five years ago

That creates hesitation.

Reviews also influence click through rates. If two businesses rank side by side and one has stronger ratings and volume, the stronger profile typically earns more clicks.

Visibility gets you seen.
Reputation gets you chosen.

How to Ask Customers for Reviews the Right Way

Many business owners are uncomfortable asking for reviews.

They should not be.

If you provide quality service, asking for feedback is reasonable.

The key is consistency.

Build review requests into your process.

For example:

- Ask after successful project completion
- Send a follow up email
- Include a direct review link
- Train staff to mention reviews naturally

Make it simple.

The fewer steps required, the higher your response rate.

Avoid generic requests like:

“Leave us a review if you want.”

Be direct and clear:

“If you were satisfied with our service today, we would truly appreciate a quick Google review. It helps other local customers find us.”

Consistency beats intensity.

Five reviews per month is more powerful long term than twenty in one week and nothing afterward.

Responding to Positive and Negative Reviews

Many businesses overlook this step.

Responding to reviews signals engagement.

When you reply to positive reviews:

- Thank the customer
- Mention the service provided
- Reinforce your appreciation

For example:

"Thank you for trusting us with your water heater installation. We appreciate your feedback and look forward to serving you again."

When responding to negative reviews:

- Remain calm
- Avoid defensiveness
- Offer to resolve the issue offline
- Show professionalism

Future customers read how you handle criticism.

A professional response to a negative review can actually increase trust.

Silence can look like indifference.

Avoiding Fake or Risky Review Practices

This is critical.

- Do not buy reviews.
- Do not incentivize reviews improperly.

- Do not ask employees to create fake accounts.
- Do not review your own business.

Google actively monitors review patterns.

If your review profile shows unnatural spikes or suspicious activity, your listing can be penalized.

Long term visibility is more important than short term manipulation.

Authenticity always wins.

Building Long Term Online Credibility

Reviews are just one piece of reputation.

Trust signals also include:

- Consistent brand messaging
- Accurate business information
- Professional website design
- Social media presence
- Local mentions

When your business appears consistently across platforms, it strengthens perceived legitimacy.

Credibility compounds.

The longer your business demonstrates consistency and reliability, the stronger your authority becomes in both the eyes of customers and search engines.

Trust is not built overnight.

It is built through repetition.

The Psychology Behind Reviews

Customers rarely analyze every detail.

They scan.

They look for patterns:

- High star rating
- Recent activity
- Detailed experiences
- Specific service mentions

If they see positive patterns, they move forward.

If they see uncertainty, they hesitate.

Local SEO is partially technical.

But it is also psychological.

When someone searches for a service, they want reassurance.

Strong reviews provide it instantly.

Last Thoughts on Reviews and Reputation

You cannot separate rankings from trust.

You might be able to influence visibility through optimization. But long term success requires credibility.

Reviews are not optional.

They are a competitive advantage.

If your competitor has 200 reviews and you have 12, you have work to do.

But the solution is simple:

- Serve customers well.
- Ask consistently.
- Respond professionally.
- Maintain integrity.

Now that you understand how reviews strengthen visibility and conversions, we move into something that builds authority even further:

Local content that attracts nearby customers.

Let's move into Chapter 6.

Chapter 6: Local Content That Attracts Nearby Customers

Many small business owners believe content marketing is only for bloggers or large companies.

That is not true.

Local content is one of the most underused competitive advantages in small markets.

When done correctly, content helps you:

- Rank for additional keywords
- Build authority in your area
- Answer customer questions
- Strengthen trust
- Support your service pages

You do not need to publish daily articles.

You need strategic, location relevant content.

Let's break this down properly.

Creating Location Specific Blog Content

Blog content allows you to target questions and scenarios that your service pages cannot fully cover.

For example, a roofing company might publish articles like:

- What to Do After Storm Damage in Houston
- How Long Does a Roof Last in Arizona Heat?
- Signs You Need Roof Repair Before Winter in Denver

Notice the pattern.

Each topic connects:

- A service
- A local condition
- A real customer concern

That combination increases relevance.

When someone searches for a local problem, your content can appear in the results, even if they are not searching directly for your business name.

Content expands your visibility beyond just "service + city" keywords.

Local specificity is powerful.

Writing Service Area Pages the Right Way

If you serve multiple cities, you may consider creating service area pages.

However, this must be done carefully.

Thin pages that only swap out city names are weak and can harm your credibility.

Each location page should include:

- A brief overview of services in that city
- Unique details about that area
- Common problems specific to that location
- Testimonials from customers in that city, if possible

For example, a plumbing company serving two cities might write:

“In Plano, many older homes experience slab leak issues due to aging infrastructure.”

That is specific.

That is relevant.

That shows real knowledge.

Generic duplication does not.

Quality over quantity always wins.

Using FAQs to Capture Local Searches

Frequently Asked Questions are powerful for local SEO.

Why?

Because customers search in question form.

Examples include:

- How much does AC repair cost in Miami?
- Do I need a permit for roof replacement in Orlando?
- How quickly can a plumber come out in Dallas?

Adding FAQ sections to service pages or blog posts helps capture these searches.

It also:

- Increases time on page
- Builds trust
- Reduces customer uncertainty

Google often pulls FAQ content into featured results.

Clear answers increase your visibility.

Answer real questions. Not hypothetical ones.

Showcasing Community Involvement

Local SEO is not just technical.

It is relational.

If your business sponsors:

- Youth sports teams
- Local events

- Community charities
- School programs

Document it.

Create a blog post.
Add photos.
Mention the event.

This does two things:

1. Strengthens your brand locally
2. Creates opportunities for local backlinks and mentions

When local organizations link back to your website, your authority grows.

Community visibility supports digital visibility.

How Content Builds Authority Over Time

Content compounds.

One article may not drastically change your rankings.

But consistent, strategic content builds:

- Topical authority
- Internal linking strength
- Keyword diversity
- Trust signals

Google favors businesses that demonstrate expertise.

If your website clearly shows that you understand your industry and your local market, that strengthens your credibility.

Content also supports your service pages.

When you link from blog articles to your main service pages, you reinforce relevance.

That internal structure matters.

Authority is built in layers.

Avoiding Common Local Content Mistakes

Let's simplify what not to do:

- Do not copy competitor content
- Do not create thin, low value articles
- Do not publish generic content without local context
- Do not ignore internal linking

Local content should feel grounded.

It should reflect real local knowledge.

If someone reads your article, they should feel like it was written by a business that actually operates in that city.

Authenticity is difficult to fake.

Last Thoughts on Local Content

Local content is not about becoming a full time publisher.

It is about strategic expansion.

Every piece of content should serve one of three purposes:

- Answer a customer question
- Reinforce a service
- Strengthen geographic relevance

When done consistently, content supports everything else you are building.

Your Google Business Profile attracts attention.
Your website structure organizes it.
Your content deepens authority.

Now that your content strategy is clear, we move into something that strengthens consistency across the web:

Local citations and directory listings.

Let's move into Chapter 7.

Chapter 7: Local Citations and Directory Listings

If your website is your headquarters, citations are your footprint.

Local citations are online mentions of your business name, address, and phone number. Often referred to as NAP information.

They appear across directories, listing platforms, and local websites.

While citations alone will not guarantee top rankings, inconsistency can absolutely hurt you.

Local SEO rewards clarity and consistency across the web.

Let's break this down properly.

What Citations Are and Why They Matter

A citation is any online mention of your business's core contact information.

This includes platforms like:

- Yelp
- Bing Places
- Apple Maps
- Yellow Pages

- Industry specific directories

When Google sees consistent business information across multiple trusted platforms, it gains confidence.

Confidence strengthens rankings.

If Google sees conflicting information, such as:

- Different phone numbers
- Slightly different business names
- Outdated addresses

It creates uncertainty.

Uncertainty weakens trust signals.

Citations are not flashy.

But they are foundational.

NAP Consistency Explained

NAP stands for:

- Name
- Address
- Phone number

Your NAP must be identical everywhere.

That includes:

- Spelling
- Abbreviations
- Suite numbers
- Formatting

For example:

"123 Main Street, Suite 200"
is different from
"123 Main St Ste 200"

While these seem minor to humans, consistency removes ambiguity for search engines.

Also avoid variations of your business name such as:

"Smith Plumbing"
"Smith Plumbing LLC"
"Smith Plumbing and Drain Services"

Pick one official version and use it everywhere.

Consistency strengthens authority.

The Most Important Directories to Claim

Not all directories carry equal weight.

Focus first on major platforms:

- Google Business Profile
- Bing Places

- Apple Maps
- Yelp
- Facebook

Then move into industry specific directories relevant to your niche.

For example:

- Avvo for attorneys
- Healthgrades for medical professionals
- Houzz for contractors

Quality matters more than quantity.

Do not chase hundreds of low quality directories.

Strong, reputable platforms are more valuable.

Fixing Incorrect Listings

Many businesses discover that incorrect listings already exist.

These can include:

- Old phone numbers
- Previous addresses
- Misspelled business names

You must correct them.

Search your business name and review what appears.

If outdated information is live, update or request removal.

The longer incorrect information remains active, the more confusion it creates.

Fixing citations is not exciting work.

But it is necessary work.

Avoiding Low Quality Directory Spam

Be careful of services promising:

"Submit your business to 500 directories instantly."

Mass submissions to low quality sites often create:

- Duplicate listings
- Spam signals
- Inconsistent information

This can do more harm than good.

Focus on relevance.

If a directory serves your local community or industry, it is likely valuable.

If it looks outdated, cluttered, or spam filled, avoid it.

How Citations Strengthen Local Authority

Citations function as validation.

When Google sees your business consistently referenced across trusted sources, it reinforces legitimacy.

Think of citations as digital confirmations that your business exists where it says it does.

Combined with:

- Reviews
- Website authority
- Google Business Profile optimization

Citations complete the ecosystem.

Authority is built through alignment.

Last Thoughts on Citations

Citations are not glamorous.

They do not generate excitement.

But they generate stability.

Local SEO is not about shortcuts.

It is about reinforcing your presence across multiple signals.

When your business information is accurate everywhere, you eliminate confusion.

When you eliminate confusion, you increase trust.

And when you increase trust, rankings improve naturally.

Now that your business information is consistent across the web, we move into something that further strengthens authority:

Link building for local businesses.

Let's move into Chapter 8.

Chapter 8: Simple Link Building for Local Businesses

If citations validate your business information, backlinks validate your authority.

Backlinks are links from other websites pointing to your website.

In simple terms, when another site links to you, it signals:

"This business is worth referencing."

Google interprets those signals as trust indicators.

The stronger and more relevant the linking website, the more powerful the signal.

For small local businesses, link building does not need to be complicated.

It needs to be strategic and authentic.

What Backlinks Are and Why They Matter

A backlink is simply a clickable link from one website to another.

For example, if a local news site mentions your business and links to your website, that is a backlink.

Backlinks influence:

- Domain authority
- Organic rankings
- Local authority
- Overall credibility

Google views backlinks as endorsements.

Not all endorsements are equal.

A link from a respected local newspaper carries far more weight than a link from an unknown directory.

Quality always outweighs quantity.

Authority flows through links.

Earning Links From Local Partnerships

One of the easiest ways to build links as a small business is through relationships you already have.

Think about:

- Suppliers
- Vendors
- Contractors
- Business associations
- Networking groups

If you are listed as a partner, member, or vendor on their website, ask if they can include a link to your website.

Many organizations have:

- Member directories
- Partner pages
- Sponsor sections

These are natural link opportunities.

They are relevant.
They are local.
They are trusted.

Relationship based link building is sustainable.

Sponsorships and Community Events

If you sponsor:

- Youth sports teams
- Charity events
- School programs
- Community fundraisers

Request a link from the event website.

Many local events publish sponsor pages.

Those links:

- Strengthen local authority
- Demonstrate community involvement
- Reinforce geographic relevance

You are already investing in the community.

Make sure your digital presence reflects that involvement.

Offline involvement can support online visibility.

Local Press and Media Opportunities

Local news coverage can generate powerful backlinks.

You do not need a major feature story.

Even smaller opportunities can work, such as:

- Opening a new location
- Launching a new service
- Participating in a community initiative
- Offering expert commentary on a local issue

Send a simple press release to local news outlets.

Keep it factual and concise.

Journalists are more likely to feature businesses that contribute to the community or provide helpful insights.

A single link from a reputable local news site can carry significant weight.

Safe Link Building Practices

Avoid shortcuts.

Do not buy backlinks.
Do not participate in link exchange schemes.
Do not use automated link building software.

Google's algorithm is sophisticated.

Manipulative link practices often result in penalties or ranking loss.

Instead, focus on:

- Relevance
- Relationships
- Real world connections
- Local authority

If a link makes sense for users, it likely makes sense for search engines.

Internal Linking Matters Too

External backlinks are powerful.

But internal links also matter.

Internal linking means connecting related pages on your own website.

For example:

- A blog post about roof repair should link to your main roof repair service page.

- A page about emergency plumbing should link to your contact page.

Internal links:

- Distribute authority across your site
- Reinforce topical relevance
- Improve user navigation

A well structured website amplifies the impact of backlinks.

Last Thoughts on Link Building

Link building does not need to feel technical or intimidating.

For small local businesses, it often comes down to this:

- Build real relationships
- Participate in your community
- Earn mentions naturally

Every strong backlink strengthens your digital footprint.

Authority compounds over time.

You do not need hundreds of links.

You need relevant, trusted links that reinforce your presence in your local market.

Now that your authority signals are strengthening, the next step is learning how to measure results without becoming overwhelmed by data.

Let's move into Chapter 9.

Chapter 9: Tracking Results Without Getting Overwhelmed

One of the fastest ways to abandon SEO is to drown in data.

There are dashboards.
There are graphs.
There are metrics with confusing names.

Most small business owners open analytics tools once, feel overwhelmed, and never return.

That is unnecessary.

You do not need to track everything.

You need to track what matters.

Let's simplify this.

Basic Metrics Every Business Owner Should Watch

Forget vanity metrics.

Focus on indicators that connect to real business activity.

Start with:

- Website traffic
- Phone calls
- Direction requests

- Form submissions
- Keyword visibility for core services

If traffic increases but calls do not, something is wrong.

If calls increase but rankings remain stable, your conversion strategy may be improving.

SEO is not just about traffic.

It is about outcomes.

Understanding Impressions, Clicks, and Calls

Let's define three important metrics clearly.

Impressions mean your business appeared in search results.
Clicks mean someone clicked your listing or website.
Calls mean someone contacted you directly.

High impressions with low clicks may indicate:

- Weak title tags
- Poor meta descriptions
- Weak review profile

High clicks with low calls may indicate:

- Weak calls to action
- Poor website experience
- Pricing concerns

Patterns matter more than single data points.

Think in terms of progression.

Visibility leads to engagement.
Engagement leads to action.

Using Google Search Console

Google Search Console shows you:

- Which keywords bring traffic
- How many impressions you receive
- Your average position in search results
- Which pages get the most clicks

This tool helps you understand what Google sees.

For example, you may discover:

- A service page ranking on page two
- A blog post receiving unexpected impressions
- Keywords you did not intentionally target

That information allows you to adjust and improve.

You do not need to check this daily.

Once per month is enough for most local businesses.

Using Google Business Profile Insights

Your Google Business Profile provides valuable data.

You can see:

- How many people found you via search
- How many requested directions
- How many called directly from your listing
- Which queries triggered your profile

This data directly reflects local visibility.

If direction requests increase month over month, that is progress.

If calls increase steadily, your optimization is working.

Track trends, not daily fluctuations.

Measuring Real World Impact

Ultimately, SEO success is measured offline.

Ask new customers:

"How did you find us?"

Track the answers.

If you begin hearing:

"I found you on Google."
"You showed up when I searched near me."

That is confirmation.

SEO improvements should align with:

- Increased inquiries
- Increased booked jobs
- Increased revenue

Rankings are important.

Revenue is more important.

Setting Realistic Expectations

Local SEO is not instant.

You may see early improvements in:

- Profile completeness
- Review growth
- Minor ranking shifts

But significant movement often takes weeks or months.

Consistency is key.

If you update your website, improve your profile, gather reviews, and strengthen citations, momentum builds gradually.

Do not expect overnight dominance.

Expect steady improvement.

Avoiding Data Paralysis

Too much analysis leads to inaction.

Pick a simple routine:

Once per month:

- Check website traffic
- Review Google Business Profile insights
- Monitor core keyword rankings
- Compare call volume

If trends are positive, continue.
If trends stall, revisit earlier chapters.

SEO is iterative.

Last Thoughts on Tracking Results

Data should guide you.

It should not intimidate you.

You do not need advanced analytics degrees to succeed with local SEO.

You need:

- Clarity
- Consistency
- Patience

When you track meaningful metrics and ignore noise, you maintain focus.

Now that you understand how to measure performance, we will address something equally important:

The common mistakes that quietly damage local SEO progress.

Let's move into Chapter 10.

Chapter 10: Common Local SEO Mistakes to Avoid

Local SEO is often less about what you do right and more about what you avoid doing wrong.

Many small business owners unknowingly sabotage their own visibility.

Not because they are careless.

But because they are misinformed.

This chapter will help you identify the quiet mistakes that weaken rankings over time.

Clarity and discipline prevent damage.

Ignoring Your Google Business Profile

Some businesses claim their profile once and never touch it again.

That is a mistake.

An inactive profile signals stagnation.

If your hours are outdated, photos are old, or reviews go unanswered, your profile looks neglected.

Google favors active businesses.

- Update photos periodically.
- Respond to reviews consistently.
- Confirm your information is accurate.

Your Google Business Profile is not a one time setup.

It is an ongoing asset.

Targeting Keywords That Are Too Broad

Many small businesses attempt to rank for unrealistic keywords.

For example:

"lawyer"
"plumber"
"contractor"

Those are broad and highly competitive.

Local SEO works best when you target:

- Service specific keywords
- Service plus location phrases
- Long tail search terms

Chasing high volume keywords without relevance wastes time.

Focus on:

Relevance over ego.
Intent over volume.

Inconsistent Contact Information

This mistake quietly damages trust.

If your:

- Website lists one phone number
- Yelp lists another
- Facebook shows a different address

Google notices.

Inconsistency creates uncertainty.

Uncertainty weakens authority.

Always maintain identical:

- Business name
- Address
- Phone number

Across every platform.

Small inconsistencies compound into larger ranking issues.

Consistency strengthens confidence.

Neglecting Mobile Users

Most local searches happen on mobile devices.

If your website:

- Loads slowly
- Requires zooming
- Has tiny buttons
- Hides contact information

You are losing customers.

Google evaluates your mobile experience first.

A poor mobile design hurts:

- Rankings
- User engagement
- Conversion rates

Mobile usability is no longer optional.

It is foundational.

Expecting Overnight Results

This may be the most common mistake.

SEO is not paid advertising.

You cannot flip a switch and dominate your market.

Improvements build gradually:

- Reviews accumulate
- Content gains traction
- Authority strengthens
- Rankings shift

If you abandon your strategy after a few weeks, you never allow momentum to build.

Patience is part of the process.

Keyword Stuffing and Over Optimization

Some businesses attempt to force keywords everywhere.

For example:

"Best plumber Dallas emergency plumber Dallas cheap plumber Dallas"

This looks unnatural.

Search engines recognize manipulation.

Over optimization damages credibility.

Write naturally.
Be clear.
Avoid repetition for the sake of repetition.

Search engines reward clarity, not excess.

Creating Duplicate Location Pages

Some businesses create dozens of nearly identical pages, changing only the city name.

For example:

"Plumber in Dallas"
"Plumber in Plano"
"Plumber in Frisco"

With identical content.

This is thin and weak.

If you create location pages, ensure each one provides:

- Unique information
- Relevant local context
- Specific examples

Duplicate content dilutes authority.

Quality beats volume every time.

Ignoring Customer Experience

SEO is not separate from customer service.

If customers:

- Leave consistently negative reviews
- Complain about responsiveness
- Mention poor communication

Your rankings will suffer over time.

Search engines evaluate behavioral signals.

Poor engagement can indicate poor user experience.

Digital success begins with operational excellence.

Last Thoughts on Avoiding SEO Mistakes

Local SEO is not about complexity.

It is about discipline.

Avoid shortcuts.
Avoid inconsistency.
Avoid impatience.

If you stay focused on clarity, accuracy, and long term improvement, you eliminate most risks.

Now that you understand what not to do, we move into something practical:

A structured 90 day action plan to implement everything you have learned so far.

Let's move into Chapter 11.

Chapter 11: Creating a Simple 90 Day SEO Action Plan

Information without action produces nothing.

You now understand:

- How local search works
- How to optimize your Google Business Profile
- How to structure your website
- How to choose keywords
- How to build reviews and authority
- How to track results
- What mistakes to avoid

Now it is time to execute.

The goal of this chapter is not to overwhelm you.

It is to organize everything into a manageable 90 day framework.

Progress compounds when structure replaces randomness.

Month 1: Foundation and Setup

The first 30 days are about cleanup and clarity.

Do not rush into content creation yet.

Start with the fundamentals.

Week 1:

- Claim and verify your Google Business Profile
- Confirm accurate Name, Address, and Phone Number everywhere
- Fix any incorrect directory listings
- Select proper primary and secondary categories

Week 2:

- Complete your Google Business Profile fully
- Add business description
- Upload professional photos
- Confirm accurate hours
- Add services and attributes

Week 3:

- Audit your website homepage
- Ensure clear service + location messaging
- Add consistent contact information
- Improve calls to action

Week 4:

- Identify your core service + location keywords
- Outline service pages if missing
- Plan basic content strategy

Month one builds the base.

You are eliminating weaknesses and strengthening clarity.

Month 2: Optimization and Content

Month two focuses on strengthening relevance.

Week 5–6:

- Create or improve core service pages
- Optimize title tags and headings
- Add FAQs to service pages
- Improve internal linking

Week 7:

- Publish one or two location relevant blog posts
- Target long tail local keywords
- Link blog posts to service pages

Week 8:

- Begin systematic review requests
- Respond to all existing reviews
- Upload new photos to Google Business Profile

Momentum begins here.

You may start seeing increased impressions and engagement.

Consistency is key.

Month 3: Authority and Reviews

Month three focuses on strengthening credibility and authority.

Week 9:

- Identify partnership opportunities for backlinks
- Request listings from local associations
- Reach out to suppliers or vendors for link inclusion

Week 10:

- Explore community sponsorship opportunities
- Submit press releases if relevant
- Document local involvement on your website

Week 11:

- Continue review acquisition
- Monitor Google Business Profile insights
- Track keyword visibility changes

Week 12:

- Review analytics
- Identify top performing pages
- Improve underperforming pages
- Adjust keyword targeting if needed

By the end of 90 days, you should have:

- A fully optimized profile
- A structured website

- Active review growth
- Consistent citations
- Initial backlink foundation
- Clear performance tracking

Progress may not feel dramatic.

But it will be measurable.

Ongoing Maintenance Checklist

After 90 days, SEO becomes maintenance and refinement.

Monthly:

- Request reviews consistently
- Respond to all reviews
- Publish at least one useful piece of content
- Check Google Business Profile insights
- Review website traffic trends

Quarterly:

- Audit citations for accuracy
- Update photos
- Review service pages for improvements
- Assess backlink opportunities

SEO is not a one time project.

It is a living system.

Small improvements compound over time.

Staying Focused on What Matters

You do not need to master every advanced tactic.

You need to:

- Stay consistent
- Stay organized
- Avoid shortcuts
- Monitor real outcomes

If you follow this 90 day framework, you will already be ahead of many local competitors.

Discipline beats intensity.

Last Thoughts on the 90 Day Plan

Local SEO success is not built in a single week.

It is built through structure, consistency, and patience.

When you approach it methodically, you reduce overwhelm.

When you reduce overwhelm, you increase follow through.

You now have the blueprint.

All that remains is execution.

Let's move into the conclusion and tie everything together.

Conclusion

If you have made it this far, you now understand something most small business owners do not.

Local SEO is not mysterious.

It is structured.

Throughout this book, we broke down the system step by step.

- You learned how local search actually works.
- You learned how to optimize your Google Business Profile properly.
- You learned how to structure your website for clarity and relevance.
- You learned how to choose keywords based on real customer behavior.
- You learned how reviews, citations, and backlinks strengthen authority.
- You learned how to track progress without becoming overwhelmed.
- You learned what mistakes quietly damage rankings.

And you now have a 90 day action plan.

That is not theory.

That is a framework.

Local SEO Is an Asset, Not an Expense

One of the biggest mindset shifts you must make is this:

SEO is not advertising.

Advertising stops when the budget stops.

SEO builds equity.

Every review you collect strengthens your credibility.
Every optimized page increases your visibility.
Every accurate citation reinforces trust.
Every backlink strengthens authority.

Over time, this compounds.

Local SEO becomes an asset that continues working even when you are not actively investing money into ads.

That is powerful.

Competing Without Outspending

Small business owners often believe they cannot compete with larger companies.

But local SEO does not reward size alone.

It rewards:

- Relevance
- Accuracy

- Consistency
- Engagement
- Authority

A well optimized local business can outrank a larger competitor that neglects its digital presence.

You do not need the biggest budget.

You need the clearest signals.

Clarity Wins

Throughout this book, one theme has repeated:

Clarity.

Be clear about what you do.
Be clear about where you operate.
Be clear in your messaging.
Be clear in your contact information.
Be clear in your content.

Search engines reward clarity.

Customers respond to clarity.

Confusion weakens rankings and conversions.

Clarity strengthens both.

Patience and Consistency

Local SEO is not immediate.

But it is predictable.

If you:

- Maintain your Google Business Profile
- Strengthen your website structure
- Publish useful local content
- Collect reviews consistently
- Maintain citation accuracy
- Build relevant local links

Progress follows.

It may be gradual.

But gradual growth is sustainable growth.

Momentum builds when effort is steady.

The Real Goal

The real goal is not rankings.

The real goal is:

- More calls
- More direction requests
- More booked appointments
- More customers
- More revenue

Rankings are a mechanism.

Revenue is the outcome.

Never lose sight of that distinction.

Final Thoughts

Local SEO is not reserved for marketers or agencies.

It is accessible to disciplined business owners who are willing to:

- Learn the structure
- Apply it consistently
- Avoid shortcuts

You now have the knowledge.

You now have the framework.

The only variable left is execution.

If you apply what you have learned in this book with patience and consistency, your visibility will strengthen.

And when visibility strengthens, opportunity increases.

Your local market is searching.

Make sure they can find you.

About the Author

Roggie (Raj) Clark, is an 10-year SEO professional and owner of the SEO agency; *Bounce Rank.* Prior to joining the SEO industry, Raj was a web developer and school teacher. It was through creating his own websites, and wanting a career change from teaching, that Raj stumbled across the world of SEO.

Since joining the field nearly a decade ago, Raj has worked on a wide range of campaigns, from eCommerce, to B2B, Healthcare, enterprise companies and marketing agencies in the United States.

He is regarded as an expert, and guru by his colleagues, and the SEO industry. Raj currently lives in Maryland with his sister and niece.

Consulting or Coaching Services

I know that from reading this book, it simply may not be enough information for you or you may require more personalized support with your unique business situation.

So because of that, I'm offering the opportunity to receive consulting or coaching from me on SEO. I can offer support with:

- Creating SOPs (Standard Operating Procedures)
- Creating SEO strategies
- SEO implementation
- Content suggestions
- Technical audits
- Web design/migrations
- Competitor analysis
- Keyword research
- SEO career coaching

If you are interested in any of these services, or would like to request more information, for a specific need you may have.

Please email me at **bouncerankseo@gmail.com**. In your email, please include the following information:

- Your name
- The business you represent (if applicable)

- Team size (if applicable)
- The type of service you would like to receive
- The length of service needed
- Any other important information I should know

My administrative assistant will email you back within 24 - 48 hours with rates, and an information sheet for you to review. Thank you so much for your time and interest.

www.ingramcontent.com/pod-product-compliance
Lightning Source LLC
LaVergne TN
LVHW022118200926
848481LV00003B/1193